Elephant

Patricia Whitehouse

Heinemann Library
Chicago, Illinois

Customer Service 888-454-2279
Visit our website at www.heinemannlibrary.com

Designed by Sue Emerson, Heinemann Library
Printed and bound in the United States by Lake Book Manufacturing, Inc.

07 06 05 04 03
10 9 8 7 6 5 4 3 2 1

Library of Congress Cataloging-in-Publication Data
Whitehouse, Patricia, 1958-
    Elephant / Patricia Whitehouse.
        p. cm. — (Zoo animals)
Includes index.
Summary: An introduction to elephants, including their size, diet and everyday life style, which highlights differences between those in the wild and those living in a zoo habitat.
    ISBN: 1-58810-897-X (HC), 1-40340-643-X (Pbk.)
    1. Elephants—Juvenile literature. [1. Elephants. 2. Zoo animals.] I. Title.
    QL737.P98 W5 2002
    599.67—dc21
                                2001006872

Acknowledgments
The author and publishers are grateful to the following for permission to reproduce copyright material:
Title page, pp. 6, 14, 22, 24 Martin Harvey/DRK Photo; pp. 4, 10, 12, 19 Stephen J. Krasemann/DRK Photo; pp. 5, 7T, 11 Chicago Zoological Society/The Brookfield Zoo; p. 7B John Cancalosi/DRK Photo; pp. 8, 9 Stephanie Maze/Corbis; p. 13 Jim Schulz/Chicago Zoological Society/The Brookfield Zoo/Heinemann Library; p. 15 Kenneth W. Fink/Photo Researchers, Inc.; p. 16 M. P. Kahl/Photo Researchers, Inc.; p. 17 Tim Davis/Photo Researchers, Inc.; p. 18 M. P. Kahl/ DRK Photo; p. 20 Kim Fennema/Visuals Unlimited; p. 21 George J. Sanker/DRK Photo; p. 23 (row 1, L-R) Stephanie Maze/Corbis, Stephen J. Krasemann/DRK Photo, Martin Harvey/DRK Photo; p. 23 (row 2, L-R) Chicago Zoological Society/The Brookfield Zoo, Corbis, Martin Harvey/DRK Photo; p. 23 (row 3, L-R) Jack Ballard/Visuals Unlimited, EyeWire Collection, Jim Schulz/Chicago Zoological Society/The Brookfield Zoo; p. 23 (row 4) Jim Schulz/Chicago Zoological Society/The Brookfield Zoo/Heinemann Library; back cover (L-R) Martin Harvey/DRK Photo

Cover photograph by Jim Schulz/Chicago Zoological Society/The Brookfield Zoo
Photo research by Bill Broyles

Every effort has been made to contact copyright holders of any material reproduced in this book.
Any omissions will be rectified in subsequent printings if notice is given to the publisher.

Special thanks to our advisory panel for their help in the preparation of this book:

Eileen Day, Preschool Teacher
Chicago, IL

Ellen Dolmetsch,
Library Media Specialist
Wilmington, DE

Kathleen Gilbert,
Teacher
Round Rock, TX

Sandra Gilbert,
Library Media Specialist
Houston, TX

Angela Leeper,
Educational Consultant
North Carolina Department
of Public Instruction
Raleigh, NC

Pam McDonald, Reading Teacher
Winter Springs, FL

Melinda Murphy,
Library Media Specialist
Houston, TX

COUNTY EXTENSION DEPARTMENT

We would also like to thank Lee Haines, Assistant Director of Marketing and Public Relations at the Brookfield Zoo in Brookfield, Illinois, for his review of this book.

Some words are shown in bold, **like this.**
You can find them in the picture glossary on page 23.

Contents

What Are Elephants?

Elephants are **mammals.**

Mammals have hair or fur on their bodies.

In the wild, elephants live where it is warm all year.

But you can see elephants at the zoo.

What Do Elephants Look Like?

tusks   trunk

Elephants are big gray animals with long **trunks.**

Some elephants have **tusks.**

African elephant

Asian elephant

African elephants have large, floppy ears.

Asian elephants have smaller ears.

What Do Baby Elephants Look Like?

A baby elephant looks like its parents, but it is smaller.

Baby elephants are called **calves**.

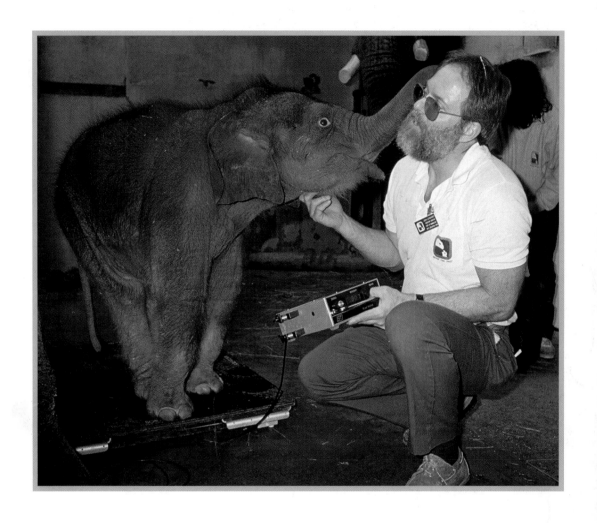

A new calf is not much taller than you.

But a calf can weigh as much as you and three friends!

Where Do Elephants Live?

In the wild, elephants live in groups called **herds.**

Some elephants live in **grasslands.**

In the zoo, elephants live in **enclosures.**

The enclosures have trees, grass, and water.

What Do Elephants Eat?

In the wild, elephants eat grass and leaves.

They need to eat a lot!

At the zoo, elephants eat **hay** and carrots.

These elephants are eating a treat made of fruits, leaves, and vegetables.

What Do Elephants Do All Day?

In the wild, elephants spend most of the day eating.

They use their **trunks** to pick up food.

In the zoo, elephants spend time playing.

Zookeepers give the elephants special toys.

When Do Elephants Sleep?

Elephants sleep a few minutes at a time.

They sleep only a few hours each day.

Elephants sleep standing up or lying down.

Sometimes they lean on trees or other elephants.

What Sounds Do Elephants Make?

Elephants make sounds with their **trunks**.

They can sound like someone blowing a **trumpet**.

Elephants make low sounds that people can't hear.

But other elephants can hear those sounds far away.

How Are Elephants Special?

Zookeepers can teach elephants.

An elephant can learn to hold up its foot to be cleaned.

Elephants take care of each other.

They work together to keep the **herd** safe.

Quiz

Do you remember what these elephant parts are called?

Look for the answers on page 24.

?   **?**   **?**

Picture Glossary

calf
pages 8, 9

herd
pages 10, 21

trunk
pages 6, 14, 18

enclosure
page 11

mammal
page 4

tusk
page 6

grasslands
page 10

trumpet
page 18

zookeeper
pages 15, 20

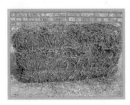

hay
page 13

23

Note to Parents and Teachers

Reading for information is an important part of a child's literacy development. Learning begins with a question about something. Help children think of themselves as investigators and researchers by encouraging their questions about the world around them. In this book, the animal is identified as a mammal. A mammal is an animal that is covered with hair or fur and that feeds its young with milk from its body. The symbol for mammal in the picture glossary is a dog nursing its babies. Point out that although the photograph for mammal shows a dog, many other animals are mammals—including humans.

Index

Answers to quiz on page 22

ear   tusks   trunk